the

ILLUSTRATED HISTORIES
of
EVERYDAY
EXPRESSIONS

the ILLUSTRATED HISTORIES *of* EVERYDAY EXPRESSIONS

{ *Discover the True Stories Behind the English Language's* 64 *Most Popular Idioms* }

by James McGuire

Illustrated *by* Alex Kalomeris

CIDER MILL PRESS

BOOK PUBLISHERS

THE ILLUSTRATED HISTORIES
OF EVERYDAY EXPRESSIONS

13-Digit ISBN: 978-1732512603

10-Digit ISBN: 1732512604

This book may be ordered by mail from the publisher. Please include $5.99 for postage and handling. Please support your local bookseller first!

Books published by Cider Mill Press Book Publishers are available at special discounts for bulk purchases in the United States by corporations, institutions, and other organizations. For more information, please contact the publisher.

Cider Mill Press Book Publishers
"Where good books are ready for press"
501 Nelson Place
Nashville, Tennessee 37214

cidermillpress.com

Printed in Malaysia

Typography: Caveat

24 25 26 27 COS 9 8 7 6

This book is dedicated to my grandfather,
whose generous heart kept him as happy as a clam

"Every speech hath certaine Idiomes,
and customary Phrases of its own."

—J. Howell, 1642

CONTENTS

INTRODUCTION

Why do we bring home the bacon, instead of some other salty meat? Whose beans are we spilling, exactly? Why was that cat in the bag to begin with? Every day, English-speaking people turn phrase after phrase, idiom after idiom, with no actual idea what they are saying! Sure, the meaning of these expressions has long been established, but rarely do we stop to think about where they come from.

The *Oxford English Dictionary* defines an idiom as a "language, especially a person or people's own language; the distinctive form of speech of a particular people or country." That is why these everyday expressions are so fascinating: They are rooted in time and place, and loaded with long-forgotten history. Many of them sound completely nonsensical, and they are known for bedeviling children and non-native English-language speakers. It is impossible to figure out what an idiom means by looking up the definitions of the individual words. Instead, one must turn to the history books.

In *The Illustrated Histories of Everyday Expressions*, you will discover the peculiar history of 64 of the most strange and wonderful English-language idioms of the past century. No longer will you wonder why getting a goat is so frustrating, or why hatters are so mad (and no, that one doesn't come from *Alice in Wonderland*)! In the pages that follow, everyday phrases come to life.

GET YOUR GOAT
IRRITATE OR ANNOY SOMEONE

GOATS HAVE A UNIQUE ABILITY TO CALM HORSES WITH THEIR PRESENCE. THAT IS WHY GOATS AND HORSES OFTEN FORM ADORABLE FRIENDSHIPS. IT IS ALSO WHY JOCKEYS PUT GOATS IN THEIR STABLES TO KEEP HORSES CALM BEFORE A BIG RACE. LEGEND HAS IT THAT A SNEAKY COMPETITOR WILL STEAL THE GOAT OUT OF THEIR RIVAL'S STABLE, THEREBY **GETTING THEIR GOAT** AND FREAKING OUT THEIR HORSE!

THAT IS HOW THE STORY GOES, ANYWAY.
THE SAYING MIGHT SIMPLY COME FROM
THE FACT THAT IN THE EARLY 1900s,
"GOAT" WAS COMMONLY USED AS A SLANG
WORD MEANING "ANGRY" OR "ANNOYED"!

RIDING SHOTGUN

SITTING IN THE FRONT PASSENGER SEAT OF A VEHICLE

THE WILD WEST WAS A DANGEROUS
PLACE FOR TRAVELERS.

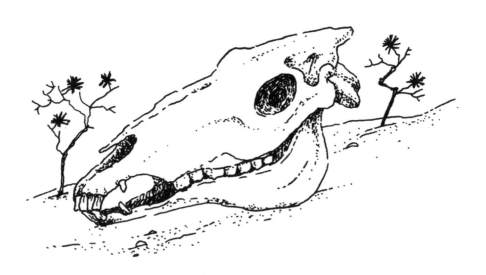

HIGHWAY ROBBERIES TOOK
PLACE ALL THE TIME!

TO DEFEND THEMSELVES AGAINST CRIME, COACH DRIVERS LIKED
TO HAVE A PERSON RIDE WITH THEM, ARMED WITH A SHOTGUN.

THE PERSON **RIDING SHOTGUN**
ALWAYS MADE SURE TO PROTECT
AND ASSIST THE DRIVER!

LET THE CAT OUT OF THE BAG

CARELESSLY REVEAL A SECRET

PIGS, LIKE ALL FARM ANIMALS, WERE VALUABLE COMMODITIES IN 1700s EUROPE. STREET VENDORS SOLD BABY PIGS IN EASY-TO-CARRY BURLAP SACKS.

DISHONEST SALESMEN REPLACED THE PIGLETS WITH CATS, WHICH WERE FAR LESS VALUABLE ANIMALS.

WHEN ONE OF THESE CATS MANAGED TO WRIGGLE FREE— **LETTING THE CAT OUT OF THE BAG**— THE DECEIT WAS REVEALED!

BUTTER SOMEONE UP

TO EXCESSIVELY PRAISE OR FLATTER

IN ANCIENT INDIA, CITIZENS TOOK PART IN A RELIGIOUS TRADITION THAT INVOLVED THROWING BALLS OF BUTTER AT STATUES OF DEITIES. THIS WAS SAID TO BRING GOOD FORTUNE TO ALL WHO TOOK PART.

IN TIBET, PEOPLE WOULD EVEN BUILD ENTIRE SCULPTURES OUT OF BUTTER. BY **BUTTERING UP** THE GODS, IT WAS HOPED THAT THEY WOULD BE MET WITH GOOD FAVOR!

SKELETON IN THE CLOSET

AN EMBARRASSING OR DAMAGING SECRET

IN PLAGUE-RIDDEN 1800s ENGLAND, DISEASE WAS FAR MORE DEBILITATING THAN IT IS TODAY. TYPHUS, CHOLERA, YELLOW FEVER, BUBONIC PLAGUE, INFLUENZA, MEASLES, AND SMALLPOX WIPED OUT HUNDREDS OF THOUSANDS OF PEOPLE AT A TIME. EVEN THE SLIGHTEST SIGN OF SICKNESS WAS DANGEROUS, SO IT WAS KEPT SECRET WHENEVER POSSIBLE.

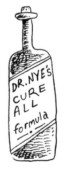

LEGEND HAS IT THAT SOME FAMILIES WOULD EVEN HIDE A SICK CHILD IN THE CLOSET WHEN GUESTS VISITED, LITERALLY KEEPING THE **SKELETON IN THE CLOSET!**

BUT PERHAPS THIS PHRASE WAS MORE TYPICALLY USED IN A FIGURATIVE WAY, TO DESCRIBE THE SHADY MANNER IN WHICH PEOPLE HID THEIR DISEASES (AKA SKELETONS) TO AVOID BEING OSTRACIZED BY OTHERS!

BITE THE BULLET

DO SOMETHING UNPLEASANT AFTER PUTTING IT OFF

DURING THE BLOODY BATTLES OF THE CIVIL WAR, SURGERIES TOOK PLACE CONSTANTLY AND IN LESS-THAN-IDEAL SETTINGS.

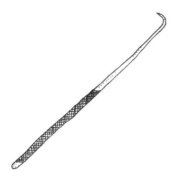

LEGEND HAS IT THAT IN ORDER TO COPE WITH THE PAIN, PATIENTS WERE GIVEN SOMETHING TO BITE DOWN ON, NAMELY A BULLET.

BY LITERALLY **BITING THE BULLET,** THE PATIENTS ENDURED THE PAIN—HOPEFULLY WITHOUT BREAKING A TOOTH!

SOME SAY THIS POPULAR EXPRESSION IS EVEN OLDER, TRACING IT BACK TO THE 1700s WHEN THE ACT OF **BITING THE BULLET** WAS A SOLUTION TO ENDURING THE PAIN OF BEING WHIPPED!

SPILL THE BEANS

ACCIDENTALLY REVEAL INFORMATION

CITIZENS OF ANCIENT GREECE VOTED ON A MATTER BY PLACING A BEAN IN A VASE.

ONE COLOR BEAN WAS A YES AND ANOTHER COLOR BEAN WAS A NO.

TO EFFECT ANY CHANGE, THE VOTE HAD TO BE COMPLETELY UNANIMOUS.

IF SOMEONE ACCIDENTALLY **SPILLED THE BEANS** AND REVEALED MORE THAN ONE COLOR OF BEAN, THE VOTE WAS HALTED!

MIND YOUR P'S AND Q'S

BE ON YOUR BEST BEHAVIOR

SOME SAY THIS EXPRESSION IS SHORT FOR "PLEASES AND THANK YOUS," BUT THERE IS ANOTHER POSSIBLE ORIGIN STORY THAT IS MUCH MORE FUN. IN 1600s ENGLAND, TAVERNS SERVED ALCOHOL IN PINTS AND QUARTS (AKA P'S AND Q'S). BARTENDERS KEPT A CAREFUL EYE ON HOW MUCH ALCOHOL EACH CUSTOMER DRANK.

IF ANYBODY BECAME TOO DRUNK AND ROWDY, BARTENDERS WOULD INTERVENE, REMINDING THEM TO **MIND THEIR P'S AND Q'S,** KEEPING EVERYONE ON THEIR BEST BEHAVIOR!

MIND YOUR OWN BEESWAX

MIND YOUR BUSINESS

IN THE 1700s, WOMEN WORE BEESWAX ON THEIR FACES TO COVER UP BLEMISHES AND SMOOTH OUT THEIR COMPLEXIONS. SO, SOME SAY THAT IF A WOMAN CAUGHT SOMEONE STARING AT HER FACE FOR TOO LONG, SHE MIGHT BECOME INSULTED, AND TELL THE PERSON TO **MIND THEIR OWN BEESWAX!**

THAT MAY OR MAY NOT BE TRUE, BUT ONE THING
IS FOR SURE: BEESWAX IS A CHARMING AND
ALLITERATIVE SUBSTITUTE FOR THE WORD "BUSINESS"!

STRAIGHT FROM THE HORSE'S MOUTH

RECEIVE INFORMATION FROM THE BEST POSSIBLE SOURCE

IN THE PAST, HORSE TRADERS OFTEN LIED
ABOUT HORSES' AGES TO INCREASE THEIR VALUE.

SMART BUYERS, HOWEVER, WERE CAREFUL TO EXAMINE A HORSE'S TEETH. THIS WAS A FOOLPROOF WAY TO DETERMINE A HORSE'S AGE. ONCE THEY HAD GOTTEN THE INFORMATION **STRAIGHT FROM THE HORSE'S MOUTH**, THEY KNEW THE TRUTH!

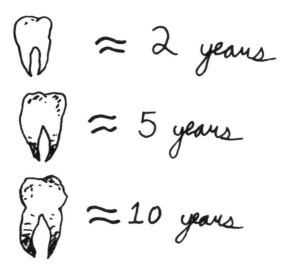

≈ 2 years

≈ 5 years

≈ 10 years

MAD AS A HATTER

CASUALLY INSANE

THE DAMAGING EFFECTS OF CERTAIN CHEMICALS WERE NOT YET KNOWN IN THE EARLY DAYS OF THE INDUSTRIAL REVOLUTION. TOXIC MERCURY (IN THE FORM OF MERCUROUS NITRATE) WAS COMMONLY USED TO MAKE THE FELT FOR HANDMADE HATS. AFTER A FEW YEARS IN THE PROFESSION, HATMAKERS OFTEN FELL ILL AND EXPERIENCED TREMORS AND HALLUCINATIONS, TURNING THEM INTO REAL **MAD HATTERS**! OF COURSE, THIS SAYING WAS POPULARIZED BY THE ECCENTRIC HATTER WHO HOSTS THE TEA PARTY IN LEWIS CARROLL'S 1865 TOME ALICE'S ADVENTURES IN WONDERLAND.

GIVE A COLD SHOULDER

SNUB SOMEONE

IN SHAKESPEAREAN TIMES, THE FOOD ONE SERVED TO GUESTS SPOKE VOLUMES. IF YOU SERVED THEM A COLD CUT, YOU MADE THEM FEEL UNIMPORTANT AND UNWELCOME.

HOWEVER, UNWANTED GUESTS WERE SERVED COLD MUTTON SHOULDER, WHICH HINTED THAT THEY HAD OVERSTAYED THEIR WELCOME. **GIVING THEM A COLD SHOULDER** WAS A NOT-SO-SUBTLE WAY OF TELLING THEM TO HIT THE ROAD!

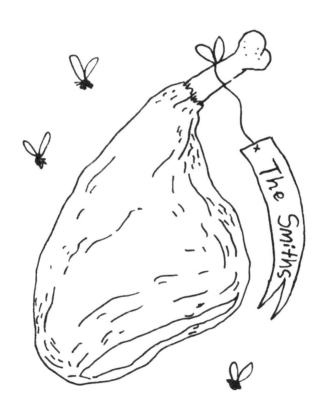

JUMP THE SHARK

TURNING POINT WHEN SOMETHING DECLINES IN QUALITY

"HAPPY DAYS" WAS AMONG THE MOST WATCHED SHOWS ON TELEVISION IN THE 1970s.

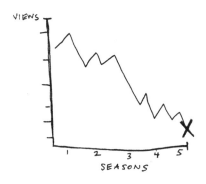

BUT, BY THE FIFTH SEASON, MOST VIEWERS WERE LOSING INTEREST AND THE RATINGS STARTED TO TANK.

THE LAST STRAW FOR THE AUDIENCE CAME WHEN FONZIE, CLAD IN SWIMMING TRUNKS, HIS SIGNATURE LEATHER JACKET, AND WATER SKIS, LITERALLY AND INEXPLICABLY JUMPS OVER A SHARK.

ONCE THE FONZ HAD **JUMPED THE SHARK**, THE GOLDEN DAYS OF 'HAPPY DAYS' WERE COMPLETELY OVER! NOW THE PHRASE IS USED TO DESCRIBE OUTLANDISH PLOT DEVICES AND DESPERATE, FUTILE ATTEMPTS TO STAY COOL.

COST AN ARM AND A LEG

UNREASONABLY EXPENSIVE

LEGEND HAS IT THAT AFTER THE CIVIL WAR, CONGRESS CREATED A PENSION FUND FOR SOLDIERS WHO HAD LOST BOTH AN ARM AND A LEG DURING THE WAR. SOLDIERS FELT INSULTED BY THIS INSUFFICIENT CONSOLATION PRIZE. A TINY SUM OF MONEY HAD LITERALLY COST THESE SOLDIERS **AN ARM AND A LEG!**

BARKING UP THE WRONG TREE

PURSUING THE WRONG COURSE OF ACTION

IN 1700s AMERICA, HUNTERS OFTEN BROUGHT DOGS ALONG ON A HUNT TO CHASE SMALL ANIMALS AND FLUSH THEM OUT OF HIDING.

SOMETIMES, A DOG WOULD CHASE AN ANIMAL INTO A TREE, AND THE ANIMAL WOULD STEALTHILY HOP TO ANOTHER TREE'S BRANCHES. THE CONFUSED DOG WOULD KEEP **BARKING UP THE WRONG TREE**, WHILE THE SNEAKY ANIMAL WOULD RUN TO SAFETY!

CLOSE, BUT NO CIGAR

ALMOST, BUT NOT QUITE

STUFFED ANIMALS AND TRINKETS ARE COMMON PRIZES AT AMERICAN CARNIVALS. BUT BACK IN THE 1800s, LUCKY FAIRGOERS WERE REWARDED WITH CIGARS!

PEOPLE TRIED THEIR LUCK AT A FAIR GAME, HOPING TO WIN A STOGIE. WHEN AN UNLUCKY PLAYER FELL JUST SHORT OF THE PRIZE, THEY WERE **CLOSE, BUT NO CIGAR**. AND ONE THING IS FOR SURE: SHIFTY CARNIVAL WORKERS HAVE ALWAYS MADE SURE THAT NOBODY WINS TOO OFTEN!

WHITE ELEPHANT

MORE TROUBLE THAN IT IS WORTH

IN ANCIENT THAILAND, WHITE ELEPHANTS
WERE CONSIDERED HOLY ANIMALS. BUT
TAKING CARE OF ONE WAS VERY EXPENSIVE.
WHEN THE THAI KING WISHED TO PUNISH
SOMEONE, HE WOULD GIFT THEM AN
ALBINO ELEPHANT. THE RECIPIENT OF THE
WHITE ELEPHANT WAS THEN FORCED TO TAKE
CARE OF THE ANIMAL, NO MATTER THE COST.
TODAY, WE CALL ANY COMICALLY BAD PRESENT
A WHITE ELEPHANT GIFT!

PULL SOMEONE'S LEG

JOKE AROUND OR PLAY A PRANK

AS THE STORY GOES, IN 1800s ENGLAND, POVERTY WAS SO WIDESPREAD THAT MANY ORPHANED STREET CHILDREN TURNED TO PICKPOCKETING TO GET BY. THESE PINT-SIZED PURSE SNATCHERS WERE CALLED "NATTY LADS."

THEY WERE SAVVY THIEVES WHO WORKED IN PAIRS TO ROB VICTIMS AT LIGHTNING SPEED. HERE IS HOW IT WORKED: THE FIRST CROOK PULLED THE LEGS OUT FROM UNDER THE TARGET, DISTRACTING THEM.

MEANWHILE, THE SECOND CROOK MADE OFF WITH THEIR WALLET, POCKET WATCH, JEWELRY, AND MORE!

THE CONFUSED MARK CHASED AFTER THE LEG-PULLING TRICKSTER INSTEAD OF THE REAL THIEF. SO THAT IS HOW **ARE YOU PULLING MY LEG?** HAS COME TO MEAN "ARE YOU FOOLING ME?!"

FLY OFF THE HANDLE

BECOME IRRATIONALLY ANGRY

IN THE 1700s, HATCHETS AND AXES
WERE IN HIGH DEMAND.

HOMEOWNERS NEEDED THESE TOOLS TO CHOP THE WOOD THAT HEATED THEIR HOMES.

IF THEY HAD PURCHASED A POORLY MADE AXE, THE HEAD WOULD OFTEN DETACH FROM THE HANDLE WHILE CHOPPING!

WHEN AN AXE **FLEW OFF THE HANDLE**, RAGE WAS NEVER FAR BEHIND!

BRING HOME THE BACON

TO EARN A LIVING AND SUPPORT THE FAMILY

Welcome
to
LITTLE
DUNMOW

IN 1100s ENGLAND (SPECIFICALLY LITTLE DUNMOW, ESSEX) THERE WAS A CUSTOM FOLLOWING A COUPLE'S ONE-YEAR ANNIVERSARY.

IF A COUPLE COULD SWEAR THAT AFTER A YEAR AND A DAY THEY HAD NOT ONCE REGRETTED THE MARRIAGE, THEY WERE AWARDED A PRIZE BY THE PRIOR OF LITTLE DUNMOW.

OFTEN, THE PRIZE WAS A SIMPLE SIDE OF BACON!

THE COUPLE ANNOUNCED THEIR HAPPINESS AND **BROUGHT HOME THE BACON** FOR THE FAMILY TO ENJOY!

AT THE DROP OF A HAT

ON THE SLIGHTEST SIGNAL OR URGING

FOLKS IN THE AMERICAN WEST IN THE EARLY 1800s HAD TO DEAL WITH AN UNRELENTING SUN.

AS A RESULT, MANY WORE HATS AS A MEANS OF PROVIDING THEMSELVES SOME REPRIEVE FROM THE HEAT. STRAW HATS, FELT HATS, BONNETS, TOP HATS, CAPS, TEN-GALLON HATS—IT WAS CONSIDERED FASHIONABLE TO WEAR ONE AT ALL TIMES OUTSIDE THE HOME.

IF A TWO PEOPLE GOT INTO AN ALTERCATION, THEY WOULD REMOVE THEIR HATS JUST BEFORE THINGS BEGAN TO GET PHYSICAL.

SIGNALING THE START OF A FIGHT **AT THE DROP OF A HAT**!

THROW ONE'S HAT INTO THE RING

DEMONSTRATE A WILLINGNESS TO TAKE UP A CHALLENGE

A HAT WAS A STAPLE OF MANY A MAN'S WARDROBE IN THE DAY OF EARLY-1800s FAIRGROUND BOXING COMPETITIONS.

IN THOSE DAYS, THE PUBLIC WAS ALLOWED TO TRY THEIR SKILL AGAINST THE RESIDENT BOXER.

ANYBODY WILLING TO TAKE UP THE CHALLENGE WOULD **THROW THEIR HAT INTO THE RING!**

DOING SO DISTINGUISHED THEM FROM THE OTHER MEN IN THE CROWD! AND SO THE EXPRESSION WAS BORN.

DARK HORSE

SOMEONE WHO UNEXPECTEDLY PERFORMS PROMINENTLY IN A COMPETITION

LEGEND HAS IT THAT IN THE 1800s, AN ENTERPRISING BLACK STALLION OWNER TRAVELLED FROM TOWN TO TOWN ACROSS THE UNITED STATES, ENTERING HIS ALL-STAR HORSE IN LOCAL RACES.

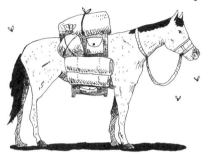

HE CLAIMED THAT THE ANIMAL WAS A SIMPLE PACK HORSE.

TO THE SURPRISE OF THE CROWD, THE **DARK HORSE** ALWAYS WON THE RACES!

AND ITS OWNER ALWAYS WON HIS BETS!

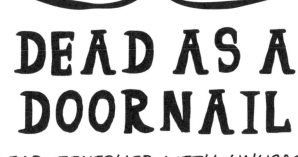

DEAD AS A DOORNAIL

DEAD; FINISHED WITH; UNUSABLE

DOORNAILS ARE LONG, LARGE-HEADED NAILS THAT WERE USED FOR CENTURIES TO STRENGTHEN HANDMADE DOORS. THEY WERE HAMMERED ALL THE WAY THROUGH THE BOARDS AND THEN POUNDED FLAT ON THE OTHER SIDE, IN A PROCESS CALLED "CLENCHING." THIS RENDERED THE NAIL COMPLETELY "DEAD" AND UNUSABLE FOR ANY OTHER PURPOSE. AND, LEGEND HAS IT, THAT IS HOW THE SAYING **DEAD AS A DOORNAIL** CAME ABOUT!

DIFFERENT STROKES FOR DIFFERENT FOLKS

DIFFERENT PEOPLE GO ABOUT THEIR BUSINESS IN DIFFERENT WAYS

MUHAMMED ALI WAS KNOWN FOR TIRING OUT HIS OPPONENTS WITH A FLURRY OF PUNCHES.

I DON'T HAVE ANY [BIG] PUNCH," ALI SAID. "I JUST HIT A MAN SO MANY TIMES HE WISHED I HAD A PUNCH."

OF COURSE, ALI HAD WON HIS FIGHTS AGAINST SONNY LISTON AND FLOYD PATTERSON BY KNOCKOUT.

R.I.P. SONNY

R.I.P. FLOYD

WHEN ASKED ABOUT THE KNOCKOUTS, ALI RESPONDED, "I GOT **DIFFERENT STROKES FOR DIFFERENT FOLKS!**"

DOG DAYS

UNBEARABLY HOT SUMMER DAYS

THE HOTTEST DAYS ARE KNOWN AS THE **DOG DAYS** IN THE MIDDLE OF THE SUMMER. THE HEAT IS SUCH THAT EVEN THE MOST ACTIVE DOGS CAN DO LITTLE ELSE BUT LIE AROUND!

THE EARLIEST USE OF THIS POPULAR PHRASE MAY COME FROM THE ANCIENT ROMANS, WHO FOUND THAT THE HOTTEST DAYS OF THE YEAR LINED UP WITH SIRIUS, THE DOG STAR, WHICH OCCUPIES THE SAME PART OF THE SKY AS THE SUN.

KICK THE BUCKET

DIE

SURPRISE, SURPRISE, THE ORIGIN OF THIS SAYING IS NOT A PRETTY ONE! IN 1500s ENGLAND, THE WORD "BUCKET" HAD A SECOND MEANING: IT REFERRED TO A BEAM USED FOR HANGING ITEMS, AMONG WHICH WERE ANIMALS HUNG BY THEIR FEET FOR SLAUGHTER. THE ANIMALS WERE LIKELY TO STRUGGLE BEFORE BEING KILLED, THEREBY **KICKING THE BUCKET!**

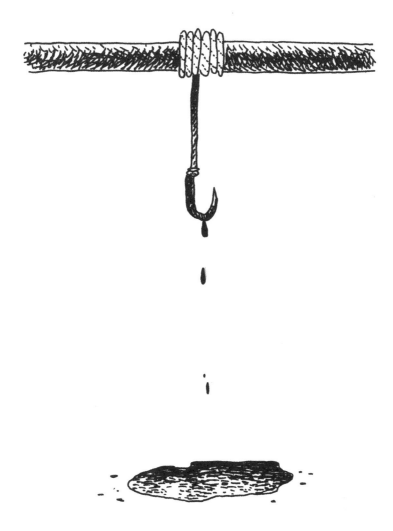

KNOW THE ROPES

UNDERSTAND THE CUSTOMARY WAY OF DOING SOMETHING

FROM THE 1500s TO THE MID-1800s, INTERNATIONAL TRADE AND NAVAL WARFARE WERE DOMINATED BY SAILING SHIPS. THIS SEAFARING ERA IS OFTEN REFERRED TO AS THE AGE OF SAIL! AN INTENSE UNDERSTANDING OF MARITIME CUSTOM WHEN WORKING ON A SAILING SHIP WAS ESSENTIAL IN INSURING SAFETY AND EFFICIENCY. SO, TO **KNOW THE ROPES** WAS TO BE ABLE TO OPERATE A SHIP AND ITS SAIL! TODAY, THIS POPULAR PHRASE IS USED TO DESCRIBE AN EXPERT IN ANY FIELD.

LET THEM EAT CAKE

SCREW THEM

QUEEN MARIE ANTOINETTE WAS THE LAST QUEEN OF FRANCE BEFORE THE FRENCH REVOLUTION. SHE AND HER COHORT WERE KNOWN FOR SPENDING OODLES OF FRANCS ON LAVISH PARTIES, GAMBLING, AND POUFY 3-FOOT-TALL HAIRSTYLES.

AMONG THE CAUSES FOR THE REVOLUTION WAS A FAMINE AMONG THE LOWER CLASSES DUE TO GRAIN SHORTAGES.

WHEN INFORMED THAT MOST OF FRANCE HAD NO BREAD TO EAT, MARIE ANTOINETTE IS SAID TO HAVE REPLIED, "THEN LET THEM EAT BRIOCHE!" WHICH GOT AMERICANIZED AS "LET THEM EAT CAKE!"

IN FACT, HISTORY BOOKS INDICATE THAT IT MAY HAVE BEEN SOME OTHER FRENCH ROYAL WHO UTTERED THIS FAMOUS EXPRESSION. WHOEVER COINED IT, **LET THEM EAT CAKE** IS ONE OF THE CRUELEST EVERYDAY EXPRESSIONS.

LONG IN THE TOOTH

OLD, ANCIENT, GERIATRIC

UNLESS TRACKED FROM BIRTH, THE AGES OF CERTAIN ANIMALS CAN BE DIFFICULT TO DETERMINE. ONE SUCH METHOD OF FIGURING OUT THE AGE OF THE HORSE IS TO LOOK AT ITS TEETH, SINCE THEY CONTINUE TO GROW WITH AGE. THEREFORE, CALLING A HORSE **LONG IN THE TOOTH** IS THE SAME AS CALLING IT OLD!

RAINING CATS AND DOGS

HEAVY PRECIPITATION

IT WAS SAID THAT THE NORDIC STORM GOD ODIN WAS ACCOMPANIED BY CATS AND DOGS. IN NORSE MYTHOLOGY, DOGS REPRESENTED WIND AND CATS REPRESENTED WIND AND HEAVY RAIN. WHEN IT WAS RAINING HARD, IT WAS SAID THAT ODIN'S CATS AND DOGS WERE PLAYING OUTSIDE! THAT SAID, **RAINING CATS AND DOGS** IS AN OLD SAYING, AND THE FIGHTING BETWEEN A CAT AND A DOG SERVES AS AN APT METAPHOR FOR STORMY WEATHER, IN ANY CULTURE!

SAVED BY THE BELL

RESCUED AT THE LAST MINUTE

BEING BURIED ALIVE WAS A LEGITIMATE FEAR IN THE 1800s, WHEN PLAGUE AND OTHER HORRIFIC ILLNESSES MADE DEATH DIFFICULT TO DETERMINE.

TO AVOID SUCH
FATES, PEOPLE
BURIED THEIR
LOVED ONES WITH
BELL ROPES.

IF THE PERSON THOUGHT
DEAD WOKE UP INSIDE OF THE
COFFIN, THEY COULD RING THE
BELL AND BE DUG UP, THUS
BEING **SAVED BY THE BELL**.

THAT CREEPY TALE MAY BE
TRUE. BUT IT IS ALSO POSSIBLE
THAT THE SAYING BECAME
POPULAR IN THE BOXING RING,
WHEN THE LOSING BOXER WAS
SAVED BY THE BELL AT THE
END OF EACH ROUND!

UPPER CRUST
OF SUPERIOR STATUS

FOR CENTURIES, EUROPEAN FAMILIES MADE SURE TO HONOR THEIR DINNER GUESTS BY ACKNOWLEDGING THEIR STATUS. AT DINNER, THE HOST DIVIDED THE LOAF OF BREAD ACCORDING TO STATUS. THE LOWLY WORKERS AND SERVANTS GOT THE BOTTOM OF THE LOAF, THE FAMILY GOT THE MIDDLE, AND THE GUESTS GOT THE CHOICEST PIECE: **THE UPPER CRUST**!

WHILE THAT TALE MAY BE TRUE, HERE IS ANOTHER POSSIBLE ORIGIN FOR THIS SAYING:

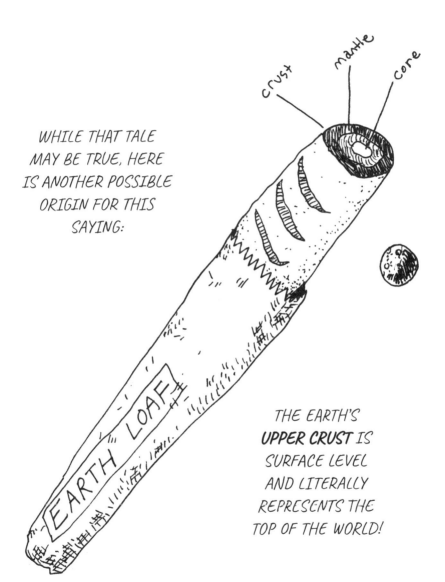

crust

mantle

core

EARTH LOAF

THE EARTH'S **UPPER CRUST** IS SURFACE LEVEL AND LITERALLY REPRESENTS THE TOP OF THE WORLD!

BURY YOUR HEAD IN THE SAND

AVOID A PROBLEM

OSTRICHES ON THE AFRICAN SAVANNA OFTEN ENCOUNTER FEROCIOUS PREDATORS LIKE CHEETAHS, LIONS, AND LEOPARDS.

THESE MEAT-EATERS ARE AMONG THE FASTEST ON EARTH, AND OSTRICHES ARE JUST GOOFY-LOOKING FLIGHTLESS BIRDS THAT LACK SUFFICIENT MEANS TO RUN AWAY.

SO THEIR NATURAL REACTION IS TO HIDE FROM PREDATORS BY **BURYING THEIR HEADS IN THE SAND**!

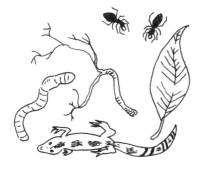

BUT NATURALISTS KNOW THE TRUTH. IN REAL LIFE, OSTRICHES MORE TYPICALLY LOWER THEIR HEADS TO FEED ON LIZARDS, INSECTS, ROOTS, AND LEAVES—NOT TO HIDE!

PULL WOOL OVER SOMEONE'S EYES

TO DECEIVE

IT WAS COMMON PRACTICE IN PAST CENTURIES FOR EUROPEANS AND SOME AMERICANS TO WEAR WIGS. MOST OF THESE WIGS WERE MADE OF LOOSE, ILL-FITTING WOOL. THIEVES WOULD SNEAK UP ON UNSUSPECTING VICTIMS AND **PULL THE WOOL OVER THEIR EYES**, BLINDING THEM TO THE ROBBERY!

WEAR YOUR HEART ON YOUR SLEEVE

TO DISPLAY YOUR EMOTIONS

*JOUSTING WAS A PROMINENT FIXTURE OF THE MIDDLE AGES. THE COMPETITION GAVE KNIGHTS THE OPPORTUNITY TO DISPLAY THEIR PROWESS AND WIN FAVOR AMONG THE LADIES OF THE COURT. KNIGHTS WOULD OFTEN WEAR AN ITEM OF THE LADY THAT HE FAVORED ON HIS ARM, SUCH AS A SCARF OR A RIBBON! THEREBY WEARING THEIR **HEART ON THEIR SLEEVE!***

ON THE WAGON

ABSTAINING FROM ALCOHOL

IN THE LATE 1800s, WATER WAGONS WERE USED IN AMERICAN CITIES TO DAMPEN DIRTY, DUSTY STREETS IN TIMES OF DRY WEATHER.

IT WAS AROUND THIS TIME THAT TEMPERANCE ORGANIZATIONS BEGAN POPPING UP ACROSS THE UNITED STATES, ENCOURAGING PEOPLE TO TAKE THE PLEDGE NOT TO DRINK BOOZE.

THOSE WHO HAD TAKEN THE PLEDGE AND WERE TEMPTED TO LAPSE WOULD OFTEN SAY THAT THEY WOULD RATHER DRINK FROM THE DIRTY WATER CART THAN DRINK ALCOHOL. THESE PEOPLE WERE SAID TO BE ON THE WATER WAGON, WHICH—BY THE EARLY 1900s— EVOLVED INTO **ON THE WAGON**!

THE WHOLE NINE YARDS

ALL OF SOMETHING

THE .50 CALIBER MACHINE GUNS USED DURING WORLD WAR II EMPLOYED 27-FOOT AMMUNITION BELTS. THE LONGER THE AMMUNITION BELT, THE LESS TIME WAS WASTED RELOADING THE WEAPON! IT WAS COMMON PRACTICE TO SAY THAT A GUNNER "GAVE 'EM THE WHOLE NINE YARDS" ONCE THE BELT WAS EXTINGUISHED.

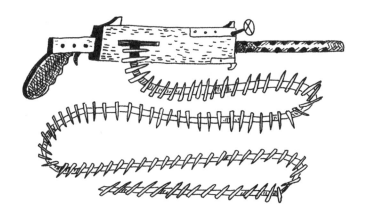

THAT SAID, THE WORLD WAR II HISTORY CANNOT HAVE ACTUALLY INSPIRED **THE WHOLE NINE YARDS**, AS THE PHRASE WAS USED IN PRINT IN 1907. SO THE ORIGINAL INSPIRATION REMAINS ONE OF THE BIGGEST EVERYDAY EXPRESSION-RELATED MYSTERIES!

CAT GOT YOUR TONGUE?

AT A LOSS FOR WORDS

THE CAT-O'-NINE-TAILS WAS A POPULAR DISCIPLINARY TOOL N THE 1800s, WHEN THE ENGLISH NAVY USED IT FOR FLOGGING.

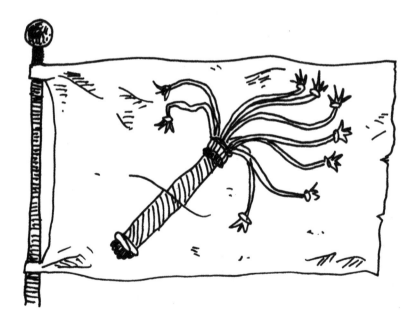

LEGEND HAS IT THAT THE PAIN DEALT BY THE WHIP WAS SO SEVERE THAT THOSE IT AFFLICTED FOUND THEMSELVES UNABLE TO TALK FOR A LONG PERIOD OF TIME AFTERWARD! TODAY, **CAT GOT YOUR TONGUE** IS USED TO DESCRIBE ANYONE WHO IS AT A LOSS FOR WORDS, ALL BECAUSE OF THE TORTURE METHODS USED ON THE HIGH SEAS AND ACROSS THE BRITISH EMPIRE!

ON A WING AND A PRAYER

RELYING ON LUCK TO GET OUT OF A DESPERATE SITUATION

WORLD WAR II SAW DEVASTATING AND UNPRECEDENTED AIR BATTLES FOR EVERY COUNTRY INVOLVED. PLENTY OF FIGHTER PILOTS LOST THEIR LIVES IN BATTLE WHILE PLENTY MORE WERE UNABLE TO RETURN THEIR AIRCRAFTS SAFELY TO THE GROUND. A DAMAGED AIRCRAFT RETURNING FROM BATTLE WAS COMING IN ON A **WING AND A PRAYER!**

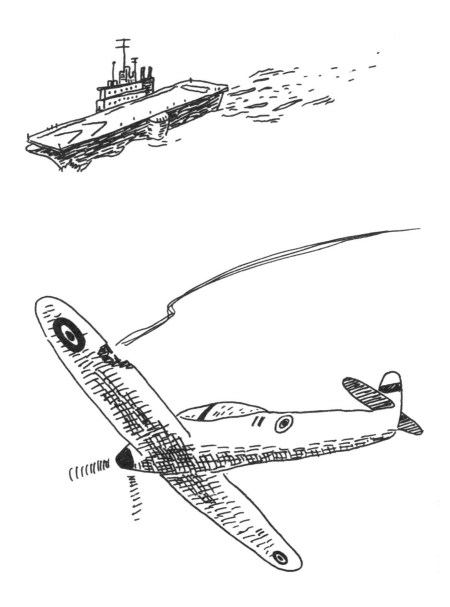

RED HERRING

DELIBERATE MISDIRECTION

HERRINGS ARE OILY, SMELLY FISH.

THE SCENT IS SO STRONG THAT PEOPLE USED HERRING OIL TO LAY FALSE TRAILS FOR HUNTING DOGS.

THE DOGS PICK UP THE SCENT AND FOLLOW IT, LOSING THE PREY—OR FUGITIVE!—THAT THEY WERE TRACKING.

THE SAYING ORIGINATED WHEN A WEALTHY ENGLISH CLERGYMAN NAMED JASPER MAYNE PLAYED A JOKE ON ONE OF HIS SERVANTS IN HIS WILL, AFTER HE DIED IN 1672.

HE LEFT THE MAN "SOMEWHAT THAT WOULD MAKE HIM DRINK AFTER DEATH" IN A LARGE TRUNK. THE SERVANT WAS DISAPPOINTED TO FIND A SALTED **RED HERRING** IN THE PLACE OF WHAT HE ASSUMED WOULD BE RICHES OR WINE!

BREAK THE ICE

TO COMMENCE A RELATIONSHIP

THERE WAS A TIME WHEN ROADWAYS WERE NOT SOPHISTICATED ENOUGH TO ALLOW FOR MASS TRANSPORT, MAKING SHIPS THE ONLY MEANS OF TRANSPORTATION AND TRADE.

SHIPS TRAVELING IN WINTER WOULD OFTEN GET STUCK BECAUSE OF ICE FORMATION.

SMALL SHIPS WERE THEN DISPATCHED TO **BREAK THE ICE** AND CLEAR THE WAY FOR THE LARGER SHIPS! THIS SOON BECAME A METAPHOR FOR GETTING PAST SMALL TALK AND MAKING WAY FOR REAL CONVERSATION.

TURN A BLIND EYE

TO IGNORE THAT WHICH IS OBVIOUS

ADMIRAL HORATIO NELSON, A BRITISH NAVAL HERO, WAS BLIND IN ONE EYE.

ADMIRAL HORATIO NELSON

WHEN BRITISH FORCES SIGNALED FOR HIM TO HALT AN ATTACK, HE WILLFULLY **TURNED HIS BLIND EYE** TOWARD THE SIGNAL, SO AS TO CLAIM HAVING NOT SEEN IT!

NELSON WENT ON TO ATTACK THE SHIPS AND, DESPITE THE BRITISH WARNINGS, HE WAS VICTORIOUS!

THAT IS THE POPULAR THEORY, ANYWAY. IN TRUTH, BRITISH NOVELIST FRANCIS LATHOM COINED THE EXPRESSION A YEAR EARLIER IN A LOVE STORY THAT HE WROTE, TITLED "MEN AND MANNERS"!

BURY THE HATCHET

FORGIVE, FORGET, AND MAKE PEACE

IN THE EARLY DAYS OF EUROPEAN SETTLEMENT OF NORTH AMERICA, THE PURITANS OFTEN FOUND THEMSELVES AT ODDS WITH THE IROQUOIS. AS A SIGN OF GOOD FAITH IN THE NEGOTIATIONS, THE IROQUOIS WOULD BURY ALL OF THEIR WEAPONS AS A SYMBOL OF PEACE. AND THAT IS HOW THE PHRASE **BURY THE HATCHET** CAME ABOUT.

CAUGHT RED-HANDED

TO BE FOUND DOING SOMETHING BAD

IN CENTURIES PAST, AN INDIVIDUAL'S LIVESTOCK WAS OFTEN THEIR LIVELIHOOD, PROVIDING THEM A SOURCE OF INCOME AND SUSTENANCE. SO GETTING CAUGHT BUTCHERING AN ANIMAL THAT WAS NOT YOUR OWN WAS CONSIDERED A SERIOUS CRIME IN OLD ENGLAND. ANY PERSON CAUGHT WITH THAT ANIMAL'S BLOOD ON THEIR HANDS WAS **CAUGHT RED-HANDED!**

DON'T THROW THE BABY OUT WITH THE BATHWATER

DISCARDING THE FAVORABLE WITH THE UNFAVORABLE

FINDING AND HEATING CLEAN WATER FOR BATHING WAS DIFFICULT IN THE 1500s.

FAMILIES OFTEN USED THE SAME WATER FOR THEIR BATHS, STARTING WITH THE FATHERS.

BY THE TIME THE BABY WAS BATHED, THE WATER WAS SO DIRTY AND CLOUDY THAT THEY HAD TO BE CAREFUL NOT TO THROW THE **BABY OUT WITH THE BATHWATER!**

THAT IS ONE STORY, ANYWAY. THE EXPRESSION IS ALSO A COMMON GERMAN SAYING DATING BACK TO THE 1500s. SO THE PRECISE ORIGIN REMAINS A MYSTERY! PERHAPS IT HAS ALWAYS BEEN A JOKE.

LET YOUR HAIR DOWN

CHILL OUT

WITH CORSETS AND ELABORATE HAIRSTYLES IN
FASHION, 17TH-CENTURY WOMEN DID NOT HAVE IT
EASY. ONE POPULAR STYLE CALLED THE "FONTANGE"
WAS A MASS OF CURLS PILED ABOVE THE FACE
AND HELD UP WITH WIRE AND DECORATED WITH
A LACE HEADDRESS. NEEDLESS TO SAY, IT WAS
OFTEN UNCOMFORTABLE AND EXCRUCIATING TO
MAINTAIN. THE ONLY TIME THAT WOMEN COULD
GET COMFORTABLE AND **LET THEIR HAIR DOWN**
WAS WHEN THEY WENT HOME AND RELAXED!

RUB THE WRONG WAY

TO ANNOY SOMEBODY

THE SERVANTS OF COLONIAL-ERA AMERICA WERE INSTRUCTED TO WIPE OAK FLOORBOARDS "THE RIGHT WAY," WHICH INVOLVED DRYING THE FLOOR WITH FABRIC AFTER CLEANING IT.

AN EASY WAY TO ANNOY THE HOMEOWNER WAS TO SKIP USING THE DRY FABRIC ALTOGETHER AND LEAVE THE FLOOR STREAKY AND WET, THEREBY RUBBING THE WRONG WAY!

BUT THERE IS ANOTHER POSSIBLE ORIGIN FOR THE PHRASE. CATS BECOME IRRITATED WHEN BEING PET FROM TAIL TO HEAD, AS THEY ARE LITERALLY BEING **RUBBED THE WRONG WAY!**

WAITING FOR THE OTHER SHOE TO DROP

THE EXPECTATION THAT SOMETHING IS ABOUT TO HAPPEN

MANY NEW YORKERS OCCUPIED APARTMENT BUILDINGS WITH IDENTICAL LAYOUTS DURING THE EARLY 1900s. AS A RESULT, BEDROOMS WERE OFTEN STACKED DIRECTLY ON TOP OF AND BENEATH THE BEDROOMS BELONGING TO OTHER TENANTS.

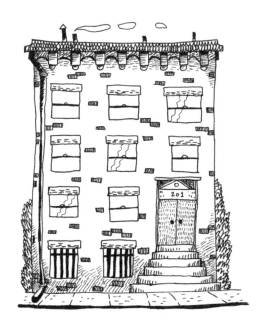

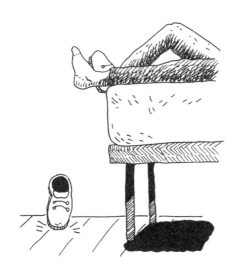

RESIDENTS OFTEN HEARD THE SOUND OF SHOES DROPPING AS THEIR NEIGHBORS PREPARED TO GO TO BED.

THE SOUND OF ONE SHOE DROPPING LED TO THE EXPECTATION THAT THE OTHER WOULD SOON FOLLOW! **WAITING FOR THE OTHER SHOE TO DROP** SOON BECAME AN EXPRESSION FOR ANY FEELING OF ANTICIPATION.

STEALING THUNDER
TAKING ADVANTAGE OF SOMEBODY ELSE'S WORK

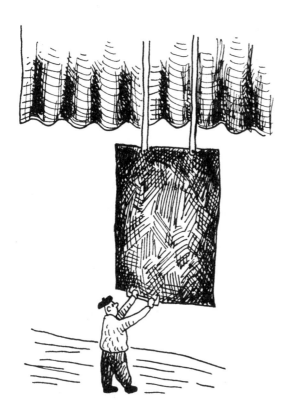

PLAYWRIGHT JOHN DENNIS CREATED A MECHANISM THAT MIMICKED THE SOUND OF THUNDER FOR HIS 1704 PRODUCTION OF THE PLAY "APPIUS AND VIRGINIA."

THE PLAY DID NOT LAST LONG, BUT THE THUNDER MECHANISM WAS SOON REPURPOSED FOR PRODUCTIONS OF "MACBETH."

NOW PLAYING

Shakespeare's

MACBETH

NOW WITH THUNDER!

DENNIS WAS FURIOUS UPON REALIZING THAT HIS MACHINE WAS BEING USED FOR SOMEONE ELSE'S GAIN. "DAMN THEM!" HE SAID, "THEY WILL NOT LET MY PLAY RUN, BUT THEY **STEAL MY THUNDER.**"

PAINT THE TOWN RED

TO HAVE A NIGHT OUT ON THE TOWN

THE MARQUIS OF WATERFORD, KNOWN FOR BOOZING AND MISCHIEF, HAD HIMSELF QUITE THE NIGHT OUT WITH HIS FRIENDS IN 1837! HIS CREW GOT TOO DRUNK AND BEGAN TO VANDALIZE THE SURROUNDING AREA.

THEY DEFACED PRIVATE PROPERTY, BREAKING FLOWERPOTS AND WINDOWS.

THE HEIGHT OF THE EVENING SAW THE GROUP COVERING DOORS, A SWAN STATUE, AND A TOLLGATE IN RED PAINT, THEREBY **PAINTING THE TOWN RED**! AND THE PHRASE CAME TO MEAN THE ULTIMATE PARTY FROM THAT DAY FORTH.

THREE SHEETS TO THE WIND

TO BE DRUNK

ROPES (OFTEN CALLED SHEETS IN NAUTICAL TERMINOLOGY) ARE USED TO FASTEN THE LOWER CORNERS OF THE SAILS TO A SHIP SO THAT THE WIND DOES NOT RIP THEM AWAY AND TAKE THEM OFF COURSE.

WHEN ONE OR TWO SHEETS ARE LOOSE, THE SHIP BECOMES
UNSTEADY. WHEN THREE SHEETS ARE LOOSE, THE SAILS FLAP
UNCONTROLLABLY AND THE SHIP TOTTERS BACK AND FORTH
LIKE A DRUNKEN SAILOR. WHEN THE FOURTH AND FINAL
SHEET IS LOOSE, YOU ARE LIKELY TO LOSE THE WHOLE SAIL!
SO WHEN SOMEONE IS **THREE SHEETS TO THE WIND**, THEY
INCREDIBLY TIPSY AND JUST ABOUT TO LOSE CONTROL.

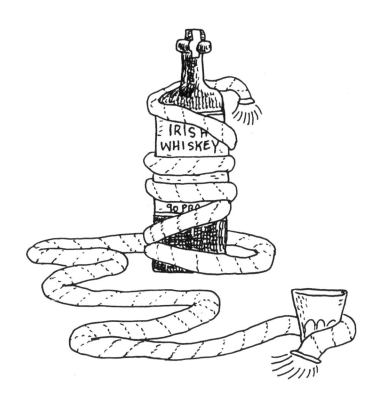

THAT'S ALL SHE WROTE

AT AN END

U.S. MAIL

THE "DEAR JOHN" LETTER OF THE EARLY 1900s WAS A WAY FOR WOMEN TO BREAK UP WITH SERVICEMEN OVERSEAS. LEGEND HAS IT THAT AN AMERICAN FIGHTING DURING WORLD WAR II DECIDED TO READ HIS LETTER ALOUD.

AFTER READING "DEAR JOHN," HIS FRIENDS URGED HIM TO KEEP READING, TO WHICH THE SOLDIER REPLIED, "THAT'S IT, **THAT'S ALL SHE WROTE.**"

IT IS ALSO POSSIBLE THAT ERNEST TUBB MAY HAVE COINED THE EXPRESSION IN HIS 1942 SONG "THAT'S ALL SHE WROTE!"

BEAT AROUND THE BUSH

TO AVOID TALKING ABOUT SOMETHING

HUNTERS DURING MEDIEVAL TIMES OFTEN HIRED MEN TO MAKE NOISE AROUND BUSHES USING STICKS AND WOODEN BOARDS.

THE PURPOSE OF
THE NOISE MAKING
WAS TO FLUSH
THE ANIMALS OUT
OF THE BUSH SO
THAT THE HUNTERS
WOULD HAVE CLEAN
SHOTS AT THEM.

HE HIRED MEN
WERE CAREFUL
NOT TO **BEAT
THE BUSH**
DIRECTLY, AS THEY
WERE WORRIED
THAT A STRUCK
ANIMAL MIGHT
RETALIATE!

PASS THE BUCK

TO PASS BLAME OR RESPONSIBILITY

A POPULAR WAY TO PASS THE TIME ON THE AMERICAN FRONTIER WAS TO PARTAKE IN A GAME OF POKER.

THE DEAL CHANGED HANDS THROUGHOUT THE COURSE OF THE GAME TO AVOID ACCUSATIONS OF CHEATING, WHICH OFTEN LED TO BLOODSHED. IF SOMEBODY DID NOT WANT TO DEAL, THEY WOULD SIMPLY **PASS THE BUCK** TO THE NEXT PLAYER!

A KNIFE WITH A BUCKHORN HANDLE WAS USED TO INDICATE WHO THE DEALER WAS.

UNDER THE WEATHER

SICK

SAILORS OFTEN FACED ROUGH WATERS DURING VOYAGES.

A ROCKY BOAT OFTEN LED TO SEASICKNESS.

WHEN A SAILOR GOT SICK THEY WERE SENT BELOW DECK TO GET OUT OF THE BAD WEATHER, AS THAT WAS OFTEN THE CAUSE OF THE ROUGH WATERS. WHEN A SAILOR WAS BEING SENT BELOW DECK THEY WERE LITERALLY BEING SENT **UNDER THE WEATHER!**

PAYING THROUGH THE NOSE

TO PAY AN EXCESSIVE AMOUNT FOR SOMETHING

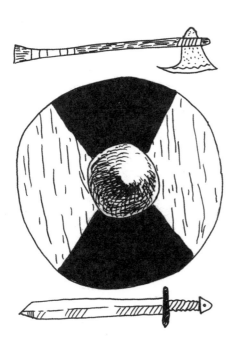

THE VIKINGS WERE NOTORIOUS FOR CONQUERING VILLAGES. THE CITIZENS OF EACH CONQUERED VILLAGE WERE FORCED TO PAY TAXES TO THEM.

THAT IS ONE POSSIBLE ORIGIN OF **PAYING THROUGH THE NOSE**. HER IS ANOTHER, FROM THE SAME ERA: THE DANISH LEVIED A SO-CALLED NOSE TAX AGAINST THE NEWLY CONQUERED IRISH IN THE 800s. IF A DEBTOR FAILED TO PAY, THEY WERE TAXED BY GETTING THEIR NOSE BUSTED OPEN!

IF A VILLAGER COULD NOT PAY THEIR TAXES, THE VIKINGS SLIT THEIR NOSE AS PUNISHMENT!

CUT TO THE CHASE

GET TO THE POINT

LOVEY-DOVEY PLOTS WERE A STAPLE IN THE SILENT FILMS OF THE EARLY 1900s.

REAL LOVE 2

NOW IN THEATERS!

AS LARGE A STAPLE WAS THE THRILL AT THE END OF THE MOVIE. THE THRILL COULD BE ANYTHING, BUT WAS MOST OFTEN A BIG CHASE SCENE!

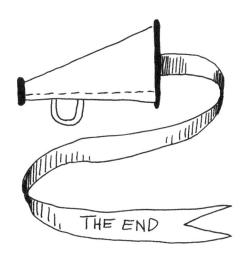

THE END

WHEN A DIRECTOR SAID **"CUT TO THE CHASE,"** THEY WANTED TO CUT TO THE ENDING CHASE SEQUENCE!

PASS WITH FLYING COLORS

TO ACHIEVE SOMETHING WITH RESOUNDING SUCCESS

BOATS IN THE 1600s OFTEN BORE A NUMBER OF DIFFERENT FLAGS WHEN SAILING OUT AT SEA. THESE FLAGS WERE REFERRED TO AS "COLORS." A SHIP DEFEATED AT SEA WOULD BE FORCED TO TAKE DOWN THEIR COLORS AS A SIGN OF DEFEAT, WHILE A SHIP THAT PULLED INTO PORT WITH **FLYING COLORS** LIKELY EXPERIENCED A GREAT SUCCESS AT SEA!

BIGWIG

SOMEBODY WITH POWER OR WEALTH

WHEN BATHING WATER WAS SCARCE IN 1600s EUROPE, MEN SHAVED THEIR HEADS TO AVOID LICE.

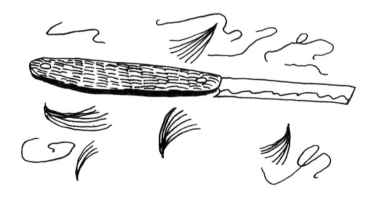

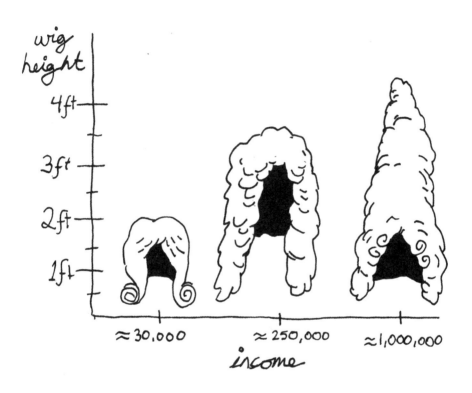

IF THEY WERE WEALTHY, THEY WERE ABLE TO AFFORD A WIG. WEALTHY MEN BOUGHT BIGGER AND **BIGGER WIGS** AS A SIGN OF STATUS!

CROCODILE TEARS

AN INSINCERE SHOW OF SORROW

CROCODILES ARE SOME OF THE FIERCEST PREDATORS IN THE ANIMAL KINGDOM. TO SURVIVE, THEY MUST CATCH AND DEVOUR THEIR OFTEN DEFENSELESS PREY.

WHILE CHEWING, THEIR LACHRYMAL GLANDS PRODUCE TEARS TO LUBRICATE THEIR EYES. THEY ARE SHEDDING **CROCODILE TEARS**, OR TEARS LACKING ANY REMORSE FOR THEIR PREY!

REST ON YOUR LAURELS

BEING SATISFIED WITH PAST SUCCESS TO THE POINT OF LAZINESS

LAUREL LEAVES WERE CLOSELY ASSOCIATED WITH THE GREEK GOD APOLLO, WHO IS OFTEN DEPICTED WEARING A CROWN OF THEM. AS SUCH, THE PLANT BECAME A SYMBOL OF ACHIEVEMENT.

VICTORIOUS GENERALS AND ATHLETES WERE GIFTED WREATHS OF LAURELS AFTER THEIR TRIUMPHS: AT WHICH POINT THEY WERE ABLE TO **REST ON THEIR LAURELS!**

BY AND LARGE

GENERALLY SPEAKING

BACK IN THE SEAFARING DAYS OF THE 1500s, "LARGE" MEANT THAT A SHIP WAS SAILING WITH THE WIND BEHIND IT.

WHILE "BY" MEANT
THAT THE SHIP
WAS TRAVELING
INTO THE WIND.

THE MOST
SOPHISTICATED
SHIPS COULD
MAKE PROGRESS
REGARDLESS OF THE
WIND DIRECTION. SO
THEY WERE SAILING
BY AND LARGE!

ABOVEBOARD

HONEST AND OPEN; LEGITIMATE

TRICKERY AND CHEATING IS ALWAYS A CONCERN
AMONGST CARD PLAYERS. PEOPLE TRYING TO STACK
THE DECK IN THEIR FAVOR DO SO UNDER THE
TABLE, OR "BOARD," WHEREAS PEOPLE KEEPING
THEIR HANDS ABOVE THE TABLE ARE THOUGHT
TO BE HONEST. THE GAME IS CLEAN WHEN
EVERYBODY HAS THEIR HANDS **ABOVEBOARD**!

ACKNOWLEDGMENTS

My deepest thanks go to **Alex Kalomeris** for his superb illustration work, and to publisher **John Whalen** and **Whalen Book Works** for being so very wonderful to work with. I am eternally grateful to all-star designers **Melissa Gerber** and **Eric Marquard**, editor **Margaret McGuire Novak**, and proofreader **Rebekah Slonim**. You make it all worthwhile. Thank you!

ABOUT THE AUTHOR

James McGuire is a writer, editor, and inveterate word hound. When he is not collecting idioms and obscure words, you can find him mastering his mini golf game or taking long walks with his beloved Newfoundland pup, Brumus. He lives in St. Louis, Missouri, where you might say his home is his castle.

ABOUT THE ILLUSTRATOR

Alex Kalomeris is an illustrator, animator, and printmaker based in Los Angeles, California. His work has been featured in published books, editorial pieces, and shown in classrooms around the country. When not in his studio, he can be found wandering the trails of Los Angeles, sketching the natural world. Find more of his work at alexkalomeris.com.

ABOUT CIDER MILL PRESS BOOK PUBLISHERS

Good ideas ripen with time. From seed to harvest, Cider Mill Press brings fine reading, information, and entertainment together between the covers of its creatively crafted books. Our Cider Mill bears fruit twice a year, publishing a new crop of titles each spring and fall.

"Where Good Books Are Ready for Press"
501 Nelson Place
Nashville, Tennessee 37214

cidermillpress.com